MASTERING
MONEY

A PILGRIMAGE
SMALL GROUP GUIDE

DUDLEY DELFFS

NAVPRESS
BRINGING TRUTH TO LIFE
NavPress Publishing Group
P.O. Box 35001, Colorado Springs, Colorado 80935

The Navigators is an international Christian organization. Our mission is to reach, disciple, and equip people to know Christ and to make Him known through successive generations. We envision multitudes of diverse people in the United States and every other nation who have a passionate love for Christ, live a lifestyle of sharing Christ's love, and multiply spiritual laborers among those without Christ.

NavPress is the publishing ministry of The Navigators. NavPress publications help believers learn biblical truth and apply what they learn to their lives and ministries. Our mission is to stimulate spiritual formation among our readers.

FOR A FREE CATALOG OF
NAVPRESS BOOKS & BIBLE STUDIES,
CALL 1-800-366-7788 (USA).
IN CANADA, CALL 1-416-499-4615.

Contents

How This Study Guide Works

Mastering Money

We love it, hate it, worship it, work for it, invest it, spend it. Money is something we interact with almost every day, not just when paychecks or bills arrive. Many of us struggle in our relationship with our finances. We want to be good stewards, yet wisdom in that area can vary from situation to situation.

While it's not surprising that many of us consider our finances to be the most personal, vulnerable topic we can share with others, the benefits of doing so far outweigh the potential risks. As we explore together the meaning and use of money in our lives, we learn from the insights and practices of others, grow through the nourishment of accountability, and discover how to depend on God rather than money for our security, hope, and identity.

Building Community

The life of following Christ was never meant to be solitary. The early Christians pursued it in groups not much larger than your small group. They met exclusively in homes for the first two hundred years or so of the movement. By meeting in a small group, you are imitating a time-tested format for spiritual life.

People join small groups for all sorts of reasons: to get to know a few people well; to be cared for; to learn; to grow spiritually. We believe small groups are the ideal setting in which people can both learn what it means to take on the character of Christ and practice the process of becoming like Christ. While there are many spiritually helpful things one can do alone or in a large group, a small group offers many advantages. Among other things, group members can:

- ► encourage one another in good times and bad
- ► ask thoughtful questions when a member has a decision to make
- ► listen to God together
- ► learn how to pray
- ► pray for each other
- ► benefit from one another's insights into the Scripture
- ► acquire a habit of reading the Bible on a regular basis
- ► practice loving their neighbors
- ► worship God together
- ► learn to communicate effectively
- ► solve problems together
- ► learn to receive care from others
- ► experience the pleasure of helping another person grow

This study guide emphasizes skill development and relationship building. It will show you how to manage and steward God's resources. You will engage in reflection, study, interaction, problem solving, and prayer. You will be challenged to adapt personal homework electives so that you can put into practice what you are learning in the group.

A Modular Approach

Each session is divided into nine modules or sections. Suggested times are allocated among the modules so that you can complete the session in 60 to 90 minutes. The modules are:

Overview: The first page of each session describes the objectives for your meeting so that you will know what to expect during the meeting and what results to strive for. You will also learn something about the author's own story as it relates to the topic at hand.

Beginning: Building relationships is a necessary part of each group experience. Each session will have several questions to help you learn who the other members are and where they have been in their lives. The beginning questions also help you start thinking about a particular issue in preparation for a time of Bible study on the topic.

The Text: Studying a biblical text is an integral part of this guide. You will examine brief passages from various parts of the Bible. *The Message* by Eugene Peterson and the *New International Version* have been chosen where appropriate. *The*

Message is deliberately relational and will help those familiar with Scripture to see certain passages with new eyes. Since the New Testament was written to be read aloud, you will begin your study by reading the text aloud. Words in bold type are explained in the **Reference Notes** section.

Understanding the Text: Unless you notice carefully what the text says, you will not be able to interpret it accurately. The questions in this section will help you focus on the key issues and wrestle with what the text means. In this section you will concentrate on the passage in its original first-century context.

Applying the Text: It is not enough simply to understand the passage; you need to apply that understanding to your situation. The questions in this section connect what you have read to how you live.

Assignment: To allow for flexibility with both group and individuals, this guide offers homework as electives. Options vary from journaling to prayer to meditation on a passage of Scripture to reflecting on a film. You can decide that the whole group will do the same assignment each week, or you can let each person in the group choose the homework he or she prefers.

Prayer: Praying together can be one of the most faith-building and relationship-building activities you do together. Suggestions are made to facilitate this time in the group.

Reference Notes: In order to understand accurately the meaning of the text, one needs to know a little about the context in which it was written and the key words and phrases it contains. The notes include background on the characters, information about cultural practices, word definitions, and so on. You will find entries in this section for those words and phrases in the text that are printed in bold type. You can scan the notes after reading the text aloud or during your discussion of **Understanding the Text**.

Additional Resources: A few suggestions for further reading or experience (perhaps a movie) may be offered in relation to the chapter's topic. At times, a quotation will be provided.

Help for the Leader

This guide provides everything the leader needs to facilitate the group's discussion. In each session, the symbol **❶** designates instructions for the leader.

Answers to Common Questions

Who is this material designed for?

> ► Any person who wants to understand better how to relate to money and manage it as God's steward.

How often should we meet?

> ► Once a week is best; every other week works as well.

How long should we meet?

> ► You will need at least an hour.
> ► Ninety minutes is best—this gives time for more discussion.
> ► Some groups may want to meet for two hours, especially if you have more than eight people.

What if we have only 50 minutes?

> ► Cut back on the **Beginning** section and adapt the **Applying the Text** section. Read the text quickly and pray only briefly.

Is homework necessary?

> ► No, the group can meet with no prior preparation.
> ► The assignments will greatly increase what you gain from the group, but they are optional.

Loving Money

▼ ▼ ▼ ▼ ▼ ▼ ▼ ▼ ▼ ▼ ▼ ▼ ▼ ▼ ▼ ▼ ▼ ▼ ▼

Overview   10 minutes

ⓛ *Welcome everyone into the group and make sure that
the room is comfortably arranged prior to their arrival. Make
introductions if everyone does not know each other. If participants do not know you, introduce yourself, sharing your name,
your role, and several objectives you have for this group.*

*If others are sharing leadership, perhaps a host or hostess,
introduce them as well. Then briefly present an overview of this
meeting, explaining what participants can expect with regard to
general format and specific content for this session. Ask someone to read aloud the text and objectives that follow.*

It's summer and I'm still paying off bills from last Christmas.
Even though I cut back this year I still used money to provide
gifts for many of the wrong reasons. To keep up appearances
with friends and family. To meet the expectations of people I
love. To protect my own pride and identity as a provider.

I hate money. It's like a beast with a voracious appetite that
only settles down when I feed it. Between working extra hours,
juggling bills from month to month, and leveraging available
resources with credit card debt, feeding the beast easily commands most of my attention. What makes matters worse, the
reason I hate money so much is because I'd love to have more of
it, yet it remains just out of reach.

Money exposes the quality of my spiritual life. I envy my
friend who just got a promotion and will make an extra ten
thousand dollars next year. My career field (teaching and writing) does not work that way. I daydream about winning the

lottery and how I would spend the money. I get confused between what my family wants—what our peers and culture tell us we need to be happy and successful—versus what we really need.

So what does a healthy attitude toward money look like? How can I use it responsibly without worshiping it or giving it power over my life? How can I release to God my fears and extremities about money?

Looking at money with God's perspective is hard work. But it's essential to our growth and dependence on Him as our loving Father. Most of us have to spend it everyday. Money is one of the foremost topics on God's mind too. The New Testament refers to money, wealth, poverty, and stewardship more than any other topic. God calls us to use it like all of His other gifts—not selfishly as an idol, but responsibly, in subjection to our loving relationship with Him.

In this session we will: discuss the various relationships we have with money, examine what Scripture has to say about the love of money, and develop an awareness of when we're idolizing money and how to repent.

▼ ▼ ▼ ▼ ▼ ▼ ▼ ▼ ▼ ▼ ▼ ▼ ▼ ▼ ▼ ▼ ▼ ▼ ▼ ▼

Beginning   15 minutes

❶ *Read aloud this explanation of sharing questions. Then go around the room and allow each person to answer the first question before moving on to the next. You may choose to answer first each time.*

Money is a vulnerable area for most of us. Our society often defines us by how much money we have or don't have, by our earning potential, by our material possessions. As followers of Jesus, we shouldn't judge each other by these standards, and yet as selfish, often insecure people, we know we do. Sharing stories about our lives and how we interact with money allows us to begin to know one another. We earn each other's trust by sharing real parts of ourselves, not by sharing what we think the "right" answer or the best Christian response is. This kind of sharing takes time but will help your group translate learning into practice.

1. How was money viewed in your family when you were growing up? Was it something to be shared, spent, saved, guarded, or envied?

2. a. Reflect on your week. How many times do you recall thinking about money—spending it, needing it, wanting to give it to someone, or wishing for more of it?

   b. Does it seem like a lot or a little to you? Why?

3. Have you ever waited in line only to realize you didn't have enough money (or forgot your checkbook, cash, or credit card) to pay for your items when you got to the cashier? How did you feel? Which of the following best characterizes your response to this situation (or how would you think you would respond if it happened)?

   ❏ Embarrassed by your lack of planning and forethought
   ❏ Ashamed of how the cashier and other people in line might perceive you
   ❏ Amused at this unexpected turn of events
   ❏ Annoyed at the inconvenience
   ❏ Resourceful for putting unnecessary items back or for finding another method of payment
   ❏ Angry for not having more money or more resources to draw upon
   ❏ Sheepish, but normal, since it happens to all of us at some point
   ❏ Other:

▼ ▼ ▼ ▼ ▼ ▼ ▼ ▼ ▼ ▼ ▼ ▼ ▼ ▼ ▼ ▼ ▼ ▼ ▼ ▼

The Text   5 minutes

Paul's letter to Timothy, his young protégé who was pastoring a church in Ephesus, is what we now refer to as the New Testament book of 1 Timothy. His main message in this letter is that the best spiritual leaders seek God. So Paul necessarily addresses numerous barriers, both personal and corporate, that tend to interfere with leaders' abilities and willingness to seek the Father first. Foremost among these obstacles are the idols that we all turn to in order to make life work our way right now. This passage reveals the love of money as rocket fuel for our self-ish desires.

❶ *Have someone read the text aloud. You may also read some or all of the reference notes on pages 20-21.*

A devout life does bring wealth, but it's the **rich simplicity of being yourself before God.** Since we entered the world penniless and will leave it penniless, if we have bread on the table and shoes on our feet, that's enough.

But if it's only money these leaders are after, they'll **self-destruct** in no time. **Lust for money brings trouble and nothing but trouble.** Going down that path, some lose their footing in the faith completely and **live to regret it bitterly** ever after.

But you, Timothy, man of God: Run for your life from all this. Pursue a righteous life — a life of wonder, faith, love, steadiness, courtesy. Run hard and fast in the faith. Seize the eternal life, the life you were called to, the life you so fervently embraced in the presence of so many witnesses. . . .

Tell those rich in this world's wealth to quit being so full of themselves and so obsessed with money, which is here today and gone tomorrow. Tell them to go after God, who piles on all the riches we could ever manage — to do good, to be rich in helping others, to be extravagantly generous. If they do that, they'll build a treasury that will last, gaining **life that is truly life.**

(1 Timothy 6:6-12,17-19)

Understanding the Text 20 minutes

4. The Greek word for contentment is paraphrased here as "the rich simplicity of being yourself before God." What do you think that means?

5. Paul contrasts two different ways of relating to money in this passage. Using the following chart, make a list of how he describes these ways of relating to money.

godly	selfish

6. What determines the difference in how people relate to money?

7. Paul describes some natural consequences of relating to money in these two ways. How does he describe the consequences of:

❏ lusting for money?
❏ being content with what you have?

8. What sorts of "trouble" do you suppose Paul had in mind when he referred to the outcome of loving money?

9. How does putting money before God create opportunities for other sins and idols?

10. a. Why do you suppose Paul chose an athletic metaphor—running—to describe our pursuit of faith?

b. What is another metaphor or comparison you could use to describe persevering in faith?

Applying the Text   20 minutes

11. a. Describe some ways of "being yourself before God." Is that something you find easy or hard to do? Why?

12. a. When, if ever, have you experienced the kind of contentment that Paul described at the beginning of the passage?

b. How close are you to that kind of contentment at this stage of your life? Why?

13. Think of people—personal acquaintances, family, friends, public figures, celebrities—who you believe actively pursue money and financial success as their top priority.

a. What has been the result in their lives? Try to consider both positive and negative effects.

b. How do these results make you feel as you compare your own lifestyle to theirs?

c. What do you usually do with these feelings?

14. Respond to the following situations. Assume that the characters here are committed Christians.

Your friend Josh travels a couple of weeks out of each month for his job. He confides to you that he feels guilty for being away from his wife and two children so much. You observe that Josh often brings back extravagant presents for his family members. Based on past discussions with Josh, you know that he works so hard to get his family out of debt and to provide them with a "normal, middle-class" lifestyle. Josh was just offered a promotion that would make more money but also require more travel. He asks your advice on whether to take the job. What would you tell him?

Stephanie, a single mother, works in the office next to yours and often complains about her low salary. It's standard in your company for women to wear stylish, professional clothes and to eat lunch in good restaurants regularly. Stephanie is no exception. She asks to borrow $300 from you to buy her daughter's much-needed glasses and to pay doctor's bills. She promises to pay you back in a month. What questions would you ask her? What would your decision be?

15. Paul encourages us to "go after God" instead of money. Reread the last paragraph of the passage. What are some ways you could focus on your eternal wealth this week?

16. Take turns responding to the following questions:

    a. What questions or concerns has this discussion raised in your mind?

    b. What expectations do you have for this group as you work through this study guide? What fears?

    c. What did you like about the discussion in this session? What would you do differently next time?

17. Read through the following ground rules for being in this group. Discuss how each one will contribute to honesty and community building in the group. Add any other rules that you'd like.

    ❏ We will practice acceptance by affirming one another's contributions.
    ❏ We will practice confidentiality by keeping what's spoken in the group private.
    ❏ We will practice openness by being honest with one another.
    ❏ We will practice respect by not speaking about a person when he or she is not present.
    ❏ We will practice self-discipline by coming prepared when the group agrees to do homework.
    ❏ We will practice courtesy by coming on time.
    ❏ We will practice listening by not monopolizing time and letting others speak.

▼ ▼ ▼ ▼ ▼ ▼ ▼ ▼ ▼ ▼ ▼ ▼ ▼ ▼ ▼ ▼ ▼ ▼ ▼ ▼

Assignment
                                                    10 minutes

If you don't already keep a journal, purchase a notebook, blank book, or small account ledger that you can write in, and put your name on it. This journal will form a key part of what you will glean from the next seven weeks of this course. For this week's session, put a heading such as "Loving Money" on the top of the first page, then choose one of the following options:

1. Spend about half an hour writing your responses to the following questions. Consider sharing the results with someone close to you. You might also agree to call one other group member during the week to see how his or her journal reflections are going.

   a. Make a list of all the emotions you feel when you think about money. Be honest about the ways you relate to it and the extent of its power in your life. How are these feelings interacting with your feelings toward God?

   b. If you were independently wealthy, would it change the way you relate to God? How? Why?

   c. What anxieties do you have about money? What fears do you have about sharing your experience with money in a group such as this one?

2. Examine your relationship with money and the ways you would want it to change.

   a. In a small notebook or ledger, make an entry each day to record the ways you spent money that day—what do these expenditures reveal about your relationship with money?

   b. At the end of the week, categorize your expenditures. What surprises you most? What other feelings emerge from reviewing your list?

You may decide to keep your list for the next few weeks and develop a budget or new spending plan to reflect your changing relationship with money.

▼ ▼ ▼ ▼ ▼ ▼ ▼ ▼ ▼ ▼ ▼ ▼ ▼ ▼ ▼ ▼ ▼ ▼ ▼ ▼
Prayer   5 minutes

Briefly allow each person to finish this statement: "One thing I would like God to change about my relationship with money is _____." Let each person pray either aloud or silently, beginning and ending with the leader. (If you would rather pray silently, please say "Amen" to let your group members know you're finished.) Consider praying by name for people in your group, listing requests shared.

▼ ▼

Reference Notes

Setting: The apostle Paul wrote 1 Timothy toward the end of his life. The letter instructs and commissions the young associate he left behind in Ephesus. Timothy faced the heavy responsibilities of any young pastor, and Paul directed him to face them squarely: to combat false teaching with sound doctrine, to develop qualified leadership, to teach God's Word accurately, and to demonstrate and encourage holy living. In this concluding section, Paul deals with riches and, more importantly, our motivation for living and our means of contentment.

rich simplicity of being yourself before God: The Greek word *autarkeia* is often translated as contentment here and literally means self-sufficiency. This is not self-reliance apart from God, but the quality of a person independent of external things for happiness. Happiness comes from God dwelling in us.

self-destruct: Self-destruction reflects the temptation for wealth to which some leaders, and we today, often succumb. This choice to gather riches selfishly—for comfort, convenience, or power—contrasts sharply with the charge Paul instructed Timothy to give to the wealthy in verse 18 (see below): "Instruct them [those who are rich] to do good, to be rich in good works, to be generous and ready to share" (NASB). Daily we are faced with choices to acquire, possess, and hoard, or to use, share, and give.

Lust for money brings trouble and nothing but trouble: One of the best known phrases from Scripture is also one of the most misquoted. Many of us have heard, "The love of money is the root of all evil," but this is not exactly what Paul says here. The Greek word *pleonexia* used might be paraphrased as "ruthless self-interest" instead of just "lust for money." Also, articles and placement are equally important. The love or lust for money is not the root of all evil, but rather a root of all sorts of evil. Our desire to use money to relieve us of pain, trials, frustrations, and losses leads to greater self-indulgence and less God-reliance. God wants our hearts all the time, and He wants us to want Him all the time, not just when we're low on cash. Our contentment depends on trusting Him, not money and possessions.

live to regret it bitterly: Ruin and destruction are the natural consequences—not Paul's condemnation—of our self-centered desire to make our lives work by using money to get ahead. Like so many of our sins, much of the bitter consequence results from our own awareness of our idolatry.

life that is truly life: The only life worth living is one where our focus is to know our Father, to receive His love and love Him, and to be more like Jesus. While the wealthy tend to face unique difficulties in needing God (see Luke 18:25 and session 3), they can use their resources to give generously to God's kingdom. This parallels the predominant biblical admonition toward money: Be a good steward because you love God, not a selfish money-luster serving your own desires.

▼ ▼ ▼ ▼ ▼ ▼ ▼ ▼ ▼ ▼ ▼ ▼ ▼ ▼ ▼ ▼ ▼ ▼ ▼ ▼

Additional Resources

Consider reading one of the following books during the next seven weeks. You may want to let group members volunteer to read one and report to the group on it toward the end of this study. You may all agree to read the same book and discuss it together at a session.

Your Money or Your Life: Transforming Your Relationship with Money and Achieving Financial Independence, Joe Dominguez and Vicki Robin (New York: Penguin Books, 1992).
The Cheap-Skate Monthly Money Makeover, Mary Hunt (New York: St. Martin's Paperbacks, 1995).
Six Weeks to a Simpler Lifestyle, Barbara DeGrote-Sorensen and David Allen Sorensen (Minneapolis: Augsburg, 1994).

True Treasure

▼ ▼ ▼ ▼ ▼ ▼ ▼ ▼ ▼ ▼ ▼ ▼ ▼ ▼ ▼ ▼ ▼ ▼ ▼ ▼

Overview   10 minutes

❶ *Greet group members. Invite them to share from their homework something specific they discovered about their relationship with money during the week, or a change they want to work on concerning their regard for money. You may want to ask a group member to recap briefly last week's discussion. Then ask someone to read aloud the text that follows.*

In Guy de Maupassant's short story, "The Necklace," a lower middle-class French woman named Mathilde Loisel dreams of escaping her small apartment and the world of her husband's civil service job. She resents the frugal budget that rules their lives, inhibiting her appreciation of beautiful clothes, fine food, and artistic furnishings. One day her husband comes home with an invitation to a large Parisian ball, and it's as if her dream has come true. Her husband even allows her to buy a new dress and to borrow a wealthy friend's jewelry for the event.

Like Cinderella at the ball, Mathilde eats, drinks, and merry-makes the night away at the enchanted soirée. But like the stroke of midnight in the fairy tale, the housewife's world similarly collapses when she discovers that her friend's diamond necklace has been lost. She and her husband search frantically, retracing their steps, their cab ride, but to no avail. They scour their apartment, but the lovely, incredibly expensive necklace has vanished.

Much too proud to admit her carelessness to her rich

friend, Mathilde embarks on a plan to replace the fine jewelry with a similar diamond necklace. The replacement costs thousands of francs, so the poor couple use their meager savings and then borrow, borrow, borrow to pay the rest. She returns the necklace to her unaware friend, and then the Loisels spend the next twenty years impoverished—both working two and three jobs, scrounging to eat and pay the rent.

Finally, one day Mathilde runs into her old friend, the wealthy woman whose borrowed necklace has cost the Loisels their lives. After initial pleasantries, her friend comments on Mathilde's haggard, exhausted appearance. Feeling she has nothing to lose at this point, the poor woman decides to tell the truth. She prides herself that her wealthy friend has never discovered the replacement. But her friend listens in horror; the original necklace was fake—nothing more than costume jewelry.

Like Mathilde Loisel, I believe many of us today—myself included—often find ourselves treasuring wealth and pride, and the illusory promise of contentment, rather than God. Perhaps we're not dreaming of diamond necklaces or palace balls—it may be a larger house in a nicer neighborhood or that new sport utility vehicle—but nonetheless, what we dream, save, and sacrifice for serves as a painfully accurate barometer of our heart's true affections.

In this session we will concentrate on why this barometer works so well and how to examine and adjust our pursuit of our own forms of costume jewelry.

Beginning   15 minutes

1. When you were younger, what was something you dreamed of being able to buy?

2. Do you think there's temptation in our culture today to resist the truth regarding personal finances? What fosters this deception?

3. In the story we just read, do you admire the Loisels for replacing the necklace? What would you have done?

4. Think of possessions or goals which are "necklaces" in your own life. Why do these things have such influence with you? In other words, what do they represent or signify to you? Risk discussing one of them with other group members.

▼ ▼ ▼ ▼ ▼ ▼ ▼ ▼ ▼ ▼ ▼ ▼ ▼ ▼ ▼ ▼ ▼ ▼ ▼

The Text   5 minutes

Jesus spoke clearly when it came to how we should relate to money and other treasures and often told stories or parables to illustrate His point.

❶ *Have someone read the text aloud. You may also read some or all of the reference notes on pages 32-33.*

> "Don't **hoard treasure** down here where it gets eaten by moths and corroded by rust or—worse!—stolen by burglars. Stockpile **treasure in heaven**, where it's safe from moth and rust and burglars. It's obvious, isn't it? The place where your treasure is, is the place you will most want to be, and end up being."

25

"Your **eyes are windows into your body**. If you open your eyes wide in wonder and belief, your body fills up with light. If you live squinty-eyed in greed and distrust, your body is a dank cellar. If you pull the blinds on your windows, what a dark life you will have!

"**You can't worship two gods at once**. Loving one god, you'll end up hating the other. Adoration of one feeds contempt for the other. You can't worship God and Money both."
(Matthew 6:19-24)

"**God's kingdom is like a treasure** hidden in a field for years and then accidentally found by a trespasser. The finder is ecstatic—what a find!—and proceeds to sell everything he owns to raise money and buy that field.

"Or, God's kingdom is like a jewel merchant on the hunt for excellent pearls. Finding one that is flawless, he immediately sells everything and buys it."
(Matthew 13:44-46)

▼ ▼ ▼ ▼ ▼ ▼ ▼ ▼ ▼ ▼ ▼ ▼ ▼ ▼ ▼ ▼ ▼ ▼ ▼

Understanding the Text   20 minutes

5. a. How does Jesus appeal to His listeners' common sense in the Matthew 6 passage when He talks about not idolizing money?

   b. Do you think His argument is compelling? Why, or why not?

6. How is hoarding different from saving? Similar?

7. Jesus includes two sets of reasons why it's unwise to hoard money. Make a list of each.

physical reasons	spiritual reasons

8. a. What do you think Jesus means when He says that the eyes are "windows into the body"?

b. Are your eyes usually opened wide or squinting? What typical attitude toward money do your "windows" reveal?

9. a. Why does Jesus say it's impossible to worship two gods at once?

b. What are some ways that "adoration of one feeds contempt for the other"?

10. a. In the second passage, why do you suppose Jesus compared God's kingdom to treasure?

b. What are some similarities between this passage and the first? Differences?

11. Do you think money is God's greatest competitor for your heart? If not, what else competes for your loyalty?

▼ ▼ ▼ ▼ ▼ ▼ ▼ ▼ ▼ ▼ ▼ ▼ ▼ ▼ ▼ ▼ ▼ ▼ ▼ ▼

Applying the Text   20 minutes

12. Think back to last week's discussion of how much time you spend thinking about money (see page 11). Would you respond to that question differently this week? Why, or why not?

13. If someone videotaped you during the past week and played the video for this group, would the group see more actions and hear more words regarding finances or regarding God? Would this be an accurate barometer of your heart's focus? Why, or why not?

14. If the passage we read from Matthew 6 was the only one in the Bible about money, what would you conclude?

15. a. What are some ways people worship money? Be as specific as possible.

b. Which of these tempt you the most? How do you typically respond to these temptations?

☐ I give in right away and move on. No sense commiserating.
☐ I give in and then feel guilty.
☐ I struggle to resist but often fail.
☐ I stand firm but feel miserable when I see others enjoying money in those ways.
☐ I pray for God's help to withstand the temptation.
☐ Other:

16. What does Jesus imply is the "cure" for money-idolization? In other words, how should we respond when tempted to overspend, covet a status symbol, or make wealth our focus?

▼ ▼ ▼ ▼ ▼ ▼ ▼ ▼ ▼ ▼ ▼ ▼ ▼ ▼ ▼ ▼ ▼ ▼ ▼ ▼

Assignment   10 minutes

Choose one of the following options:

1. In your journal this week, make a list of your top five possessions. If it helps, imagine that these are the only five things you can save from your burning home. Why are they valuable—personal, sentimental, financial, or other reasons? Does your list reveal a pattern of what you tend to value most in life? Why, or why not? What intangible or spiritual priorities cannot be represented by our possessions?

2. Spend time this week brainstorming ways in which the temptation to worship money can be diffused. Address external factors (peer pressure, culture, advertising) as well as those that spring from within (selfishness or the desire for influence, security, convenience). Be as practical as possible.

3. As I interact with my preschool-aged daughters about money, I'm intrigued by their responses and the messages that they pick up from their surroundings. One of their toys is a grocery store play set that includes a cash register that rings sales and cheerfully exclaims, "Credit approved!" when the toy credit card slides through. Because we're comfortably middle-class, my children think we have a surplus of money that comes from some hidden piggy bank. My four-year-old is just now putting together the connection between Daddy's work and its necessity to pay for our house and purchase food, clothes, and transportation. My wife and I have become increasingly deliberate in wanting to teach our children good stewardship.

But what I've discovered is that my view of money, and the importance I place on it, stems directly from many of the messages I picked up as a child. This week reflect in your journal on the messages that you received about money from your parents, grandparents, guardians, friends, teachers, and pastors. What has been their cumulative effect?

Now consider what messages you want to teach the children in your life—including nieces and nephews, friends' children, kids in your Sunday school classes you may teach—about money. What's the most important thing a preschooler should learn about money? A school-aged child? A teenager? A young adult?

▼ ▼ ▼ ▼ ▼ ▼ ▼ ▼ ▼ ▼ ▼ ▼ ▼ ▼ ▼ ▼ ▼ ▼
Prayer   5 minutes

Tell God one thing about money that you need help with—how to regard it, how to avoid temptation to worship it, how to be a better steward, whatever. You may also pray by name for the people in your group.

▼ ▼
Reference Notes

Setting: Matthew, one of Jesus' twelve disciples, often emphasizes in his gospel the ways in which Christ fulfills Old
Testament prophecies concerning the Messiah. In so doing, he
contrasts the Jews' expectations of the Messiah with the reality
of who Jesus is. In the following passages (Matthew 6 and 13),
Jesus exposes the hypocrisy of religious leaders who claim to
worship God but idolize wealth and power instead. First, He
explains this to the multitudes in the Sermon on the Mount
(Matthew 6:19-24), then he discusses it with His disciples in pri-
vate a little later on (Matthew 13:1-2).

hoard treasure: Both of these words come from the same Greek
root word, *thesaur*, from which we get our English word, the-
saurus, a treasury of words. A more literal translation might be
"don't treasure up treasure for yourself." This double reference
to the same root word for treasure reinforces the notion of lay-
ing aside wealth, stacking it up in a vault for our vain pleasure,
of an Ebeneezer Scrooge who delights only in what he controls
and saves monetarily. Wealth can clearly afford ample opportunity to further God's kingdom (more about this in the next
chapter), and He often blesses His children with material
resources, but we are not to stockpile wealth for ourselves. Then
it becomes an idol, a symbol of security, identity, and hope in
the creation not the Creator.

treasure in heaven: As opposed to hoarding treasure "down
here," where it isn't nearly as secure or beyond destruction as
we often like to think, we should bank with the only indestruc-
tible repository available. The difficulty for most good
accountants, however, lies in the intangibility of the account. In
other words, we're reminded of our need for God's grace and
our obedience to Him out of love rather than obligation or meri-
torious service. These are the only eternal assets we can be
absolutely certain of, treasure that can't rot, be stolen, or lose its
value. This is why Jesus emphasized that our hearts and the
location of our treasure are in the same place. It's impossible for
one to be here and the other in heaven (see James 4:4). The
heart, as always, must go first.

eyes are windows into your body: This passage creates a spiritual metaphor from a physical one. Just as our eyes are an entrance through which we allow things into our mind and heart, they also reveal to others what has entered in. When our spiritual eyes are singularly fixed on God's love and truth, then we are full of His light. When we "pull the blinds" on our windows—notice the way this rendering reminds us that we're looking inside ourselves for light—we experience the darkness of our selfishness. Dark is often translated as "bad"—the King James Version renders it this way—from the Greek word *poneros*. In the Old Testament this word is used as part of the Jewish slang phrase often translated as "evil eye." For example, we're told in Proverbs 28:22 that "a man with an evil eye hastens after wealth" (NASB). This reinforces what Jesus tells us here: The way we look at money, both physically and spiritually, often reveals the status of our relationship with our Father.

You can't worship two gods at once: The word for gods here, *kurios*, is also translated as master, denoting the owner of slaves, a possessor of people, not merely their employer or overseer. The New Testament frequently speaks of Christ as Lord and Master of us, His bondservants. So for His original listeners, Jesus' emphasis was clear because it was impossible for a slave to be owned by two masters. Christ made His point for the third time: You can't have treasure on earth and heaven; you can't focus on the darkness of greed and selfishness and be full of light; you can't serve money and God.

God's kingdom is like a treasure: In these two small parables, Jesus used the word *thesaur* again, this time focused singularly on God's kingdom. Notice that the treasure is not to be buried in a field, a common Jewish practice as a safeguard against burglars, but that it's found there. Similarly, the pearl is discovered and then sought at all costs. Jesus' point complemented His prior message about treasure by characterizing the response of those seeking eternal treasure: Ecstatic joy focused upon a singular purpose diminishing the lures of earthly idols.

Lifestyles of the Rich Young Ruler

▼ ▼ ▼ ▼ ▼ ▼ ▼ ▼ ▼ ▼ ▼ ▼ ▼ ▼ ▼ ▼ ▼ ▼ ▼

Overview   10 minutes

❶ *Greet everyone in the group. Invite them to share what they learned from their homework during the week. You may also ask someone to sum up last week's discussion. Then ask someone to read aloud the following.*

Everyday in our mass-consumption society we're bombarded with hundreds of messages about what products to buy, what clothes to wear, what vehicle to drive, what job to pursue, what image to create. We're conditioned to look successful if we want to become successful. From this logic, we often assume that those who are well-dressed, neatly coifed, and luxuriously transported are wealthy people. However, a recent bestseller challenges our appearance-based assumptions. In *The Millionaire Next Door*, authors Thomas J. Stanley and William D. Danko examine over twenty-five years' worth of research on the affluent in America. They write:

In the course of our investigations, we discovered seven common denominators among those who successfully build wealth.

1. They live well below their means.
2. They allocate their time, energy, and money efficiently, in ways conducive to building wealth.
3. They believe that financial independence is more important than displaying high social status.

4. Their parents did not provide economic outpatient care.
5. Their adult children are economically self-sufficient.
6. They are proficient in targeting market opportunities.
7. They chose the right occupation. [1]

The authors present a composite portrait of the average American millionaire as someone who is typically a small-business owner in his late fifties, married with three children, living well below his means in a modest house, wearing non-designer clothing from J.C. Penney's and Sears, and driving an American-made car several years old. [2]

The typical affluent millionaire stereotype that many of us may hold is now only perpetuated by those who aren't really millionaires at all. They are either hyper-consumers or work in industries where appearances of wealth and success are crucial to job performance (such as law, medicine, or entertainment).

Much of the book's popularity is its message that many of us can be millionaires with proper discipline, shrewd savings and investments, and careful attention to our lifestyle habits.

▼ ▼ ▼ ▼ ▼ ▼ ▼ ▼ ▼ ▼ ▼ ▼ ▼ ▼ ▼ ▼ ▼ ▼ ▼ ▼
Beginning   15 minutes

1. When you think of a millionaire, what comes to mind? How does this book's portrait of a millionaire compare with what you envision?

2. a. How do you define financial security at this stage of your life? Take a moment to jot down your individual responses before comparing them with one another.

b. How has your definition changed over your life's course, perhaps after you switched careers, married or divorced, or had children? Try to specify what accounts for the changes.

The Text   5 minutes

Many of us may be familiar with the story of the rich young ruler and what appears to be its obvious point. However, it's part of a consistent theme found in the book of Luke—the contrasting requirements and responses of Jesus' disciples and followers compared to those of the Jewish nation. As we'll see below, the wealthy official lacked the trust blind Bartimaeus placed in Christ (Luke 18:35-43) as well as the repentant heart of the tax collector Zacchaeus (19:1-10). If anything, the ruler parallels the Pharisees' attitude of pride displayed in 18:9-14.

❶ *Have someone read the following passage aloud. You may also want to read the reference notes on pages 42-44.*

One day one of the **local officials** asked him, "**Good Teacher**, what must I do to deserve eternal life?"

Jesus said, "Why are you calling me good? No one is good—only God. You know the **commandments,** don't you? No illicit sex, no killing, no stealing, no lying, honor your father and mother."

He said, "**I've kept them all** for as long as I can remember."

When Jesus heard that, he said, "Then there's only one thing left to do: Sell everything you own and give it away to the poor. You will have **riches in heaven.** Then come, follow me."

This was the last thing the official expected to hear. He was very rich and **became terribly sad.** He was holding on tight to a lot of things and not about to let them go.

Seeing his reaction, Jesus said, "Do you have any idea how difficult it is for people who have it all to enter God's kingdom? I'd say it's easier to thread a camel through **a**

needle's eye than get a rich person into God's kingdom."

"Then who has any chance at all?" the others asked.

"**No chance at all**," Jesus said, "if you think you can pull it off by yourself. Every chance in the world if you trust God to do it."

Peter tried to regain some initiative: "We left everything we owned and followed you, didn't we?"

"Yes," said Jesus, "and you won't regret it. No one who has sacrificed home, spouse, brothers and sisters, parents, children—whatever—will lose out. It will all come back **multiplied many times over** in your lifetime. And then the bonus of eternal life!"

(Luke 18:18-30)

▼ ▼ ▼ ▼ ▼ ▼ ▼ ▼ ▼ ▼ ▼ ▼ ▼ ▼ ▼ ▼ ▼ ▼ ▼ ▼
Understanding the Text   20 minutes

3. a. How do you think the rich official defined "good" based on his words to Jesus? How does Jesus define it?

   b. Why do you suppose Jesus deflected the title "Good Teacher"?

4. a. In light of last week's passage (Matthew 6:19-24), why do you think Jesus made selling his possessions and giving the proceeds to the poor a prerequisite for a man to follow Him?

b. Do you think this same condition is required of us if we want to follow Jesus? Why, or why not?

5. What kinds of things do you suppose the ruler was holding tightly? What kinds of things do you hold on to tightly?

6. Some people use Jesus' words "it's easier to thread a camel through a needle's eye than get a rich person into God's kingdom" as a defense for being poor or criticizing rich people. Why do you think Jesus said what He did? What point was He making?

7. Do you agree that wealth is a barrier to needing God? Why, or why not? How has this been true from your experience?

8. There seems to be a contradiction between Jesus' response to the wealthy official and His response to His disciples' question. The official obeyed all the commands while the disciples left everything. How do you live in between this tension of obedience (following the commandments) and grace (trusting God alone to get into His kingdom)?

9. a. What do you suspect Peter's motive was in reminding Jesus, "We left everything we owned and followed you, didn't we?"

b. Have you ever felt similar feelings or expressed the same idea to God? Describe it.

10. Jesus said no one who sacrifices will lose out. When He said, "It [our sacrifices] will all come back multiplied many times over in your lifetime," is Jesus referring to material rewards, spiritual ones, or both? How would you support your response?

▼ ▼ ▼ ▼ ▼ ▼ ▼ ▼ ▼ ▼ ▼ ▼ ▼ ▼ ▼ ▼ ▼ ▼ ▼

Applying the Text   20 minutes

11. a. Looking back, have you had to give up material goods to follow Jesus?

b. If so, how hard was it on a scale of 1 to 5?

1	2	3	4	5
not hard at all		somewhat difficult		extremely painful

12. Do you identify with the rich young ruler? How?

13. How do you deal with the tendency to compare yourself to others and/or to judge the appearance of success in others?

14. Does Jesus' response to the man seem fair to you? Why, or why not?

15. Why do you think Jesus asked this man to give everything away? Why wasn't the man's obedience to the law enough?

▼ ▼ ▼ ▼ ▼ ▼ ▼ ▼ ▼ ▼ ▼ ▼ ▼ ▼ ▼ ▼ ▼ ▼ ▼
Assignment   10 minutes

Choose one of the following to do during the coming week:

1. Clip pages from magazines that convey messages about what it means to be "successful" in our society today. Pay special attention to the way various ads sell not only a product or service, but a lifestyle. What's the power in this strategy? Why are such lifestyle ads so appealing? In your journal, write a composite description of a "successful American" man or woman, in your same stage of life, based on the ads alone. Then journal your response to this composite portrait. How does it make you feel? What does it make you want to do?

2. Congratulations! Imagine that you've just inherited five million dollars from a long-lost relative. Be honest with yourself

and journal about how you would spend and allocate the windfall. How would this kind of money affect your lifestyle? What new struggles would this money include? What present attitudes and difficulties would it alleviate? Would you share your news with other family, friends, and group members? Why, or why not?

Prayer 5 minutes

What do you most want to tell God after considering this discussion? What's your most important request of Him regarding the issue of mastering money?

Reference Notes

Setting: Most scholars agree that Luke, a physician and companion of Paul in the early church, recorded his gospel to emphasize the historical aspects of Jesus' life. In the paragraphs preceding this passage, Jesus is conversing with a group of Pharisees. Following His portrait of the Pharisee and the Publican, the Rich Young Ruler steps forward. Though more sincere than most religious leaders, his inquiry and response seem indicative of the Pharisaic mindset.

local officials: The Greek word *neaniskos,* used in Matthew's version of this story (19:16-24), indicates a young man under forty, who was likely a ruler in a local synagogue rather than the more prestigious Sanhedrin who tended to be older.

Good Teacher: Jews taught that only God should be called "good," not rabbis or teachers. Thus, when addressed this way, Jesus seeks to know the man's concept of His true identity. If the official is indeed calling Christ good, then he would be recognizing Him as the Messiah. Jesus' deflection is not self-deprecation or humility; rather it's a way of further discerning (and forcing the ruler to recognize) the ruler's dilemma.

commandments: Notice that Jesus cites commandments that have to do with external behavior, with violations from person to person. He saves the most important commandment, the first one, which instructs "Thou shalt have no other gods before me" (Exodus 20:3), for last because He knows the ruler has obeyed external rules but has not yielded his heart.

I've kept them all: Jewish teachers instructed that perfect obedience could be obtained through strict adherence to the Law, the code of instructions given to the Jewish nation collected in the Old Testament. Jesus turned this belief upside down when He forced people to look internally as well as externally. Consequently, hating someone is just as sinful as murdering them, or lusting after a person is just as wrong as adultery (see Matthew 5:21-22, 27-28). However, all the rich official has known is that he's been completely faithful to the externals "as long as I can remember," likely since his bar mitzvah at age thirteen when he was recognized to be a man.

riches in heaven: As we saw last week in Matthew 6, we can't worship what we have here on earth and fully love God at the same time. The two are mutually exclusive. The only true riches that exist are the eternal investments of a loving relationship with God through Christ.

became terribly sad: The Greek verb here, *perilupos*, denotes a soul-stirring grief and disappointment. The qualification, that he was "holding on tight to a lot of things and not about to let them go," reinforces the cancerous consumption of idolatry: The more powerful our idol, and the stronger its grip on our heart, the emptier we feel when it cannot fulfill our hunger for the living God.

a needle's eye: There's been some debate among scholars over whether this comparison was simply exaggeration for the sake of making His point or literal historical reference. Some Bible scholars note that the Greek word for needle here, *rhaphis*, also referred to a small gate in the wall around Jerusalem. Used for security purposes at night when the main gates were closed, the "the eye of the needle gate" was only large enough for a man to pass through, not his camel or possessions. However, other expositors point out that this interpretation seems to have originated in the Middle Ages — the word had never been used in that manner in Jesus' time. In either case, the impossibility of such a feat is the point and explains the astonishment of the disciples immediately after this remark.

No chance at all: The original word here means "impossible!" Paul uses this same word to describe what the Law cannot do for us but Christ can (Romans 8:3). It reminds us of the true point of this encounter with the rich young ruler. It's not that wealth is bad, but that being a legalist won't get you into heaven. Salvation cannot be obtained by good works. Instead, we must rely on grace, loving and relating to God as His children who are gifted by the redemption of Christ's death on the cross.

multiplied many times over: Once more, Jesus emphasized that wealth is not bad. On the contrary, many believers who make God first in their hearts are blessed with material possessions. However, this statement is not a cause-effect promise that we'll be rich simply by giving everything up to follow Christ. It's a reminder of what's truly important — our relationship with God, loving others, spreading His truth — versus the things, like wealth and possessions, that we often focus on first.

---

1. Thomas J. Stanley and William D. Danko, *The Millionaire Next Door: The Surprising Secrets of America's Wealthy* (Atlanta, GA: Longstreet Press, 1996), pp. 3-4.
2. Stanley and Danko, pp. 9-10.

Spiritual Poverty

▼ ▼

Overview   10 minutes

❶ *Welcome everyone in the group. Invite members to share from their homework, or, if they didn't choose to do their homework, ask someone to recap last week's discussion. Then ask someone to read the following to the group.*

In F. Scott Fitzgerald's novel, *The Great Gatsby*, his narrator Nick Carraway realizes that often the rich think they are above the moral constraints placed on us by society.

> They [wealthy people like the Buchanans] were careless people . . . they smashed up things and creatures and then retreated back into their money or their vast carelessness, or whatever it was that kept them together, and let other people clean up the mess they had made. . . . [1]

He concludes that grass may not be as green for the wealthy as it appears, something we discussed in last week's session. Scripture seems to bear this out as well. James asked, "Has not God chosen those who are poor in the eyes of the world to be rich in faith and to inherit the kingdom he promised those who love him?" (James 2:5, NIV).

In 1997, the U.S. government considered the poverty level

to be $16,050 for a family of four. This means that 14.5 percent, or about 38 million people, were considered poverty level or below.[2] I'm guessing most of us don't fall in this category. Even if we're not wealthy, we have a place to live, clothes to wear, and plenty of food to eat. Perhaps, because of parents or grandparents who lived during the Great Depression or economic recessive times since then, we may view poverty as the worst imaginable state. In an upwardly mobile consumerist culture, having neither resources nor power to improve one's status is regarded with contempt. In the capitalist land of the American dream, it's easy to think that anyone can advance through hard work, honesty, diligence, and godly behavior.

However, that's not necessarily the way the poor see themselves. From my experience teaching poetry writing in homeless shelters, I observed that many of them feel trapped by a culture which dismisses them and provides relatively few options for self-improvement. One woman in my group wrote about her frustration:

> Ain't no hand pulling me nowhere but down
> All my family wanting something, I'm gonna drown,
> Cause I can't find nothing to hope for
> Except a day when the Lord shines on me
> And I can smile instead of frown.[3]

Statistically, that day doesn't come for most poor people in this life. Nonetheless, and this emerges clearly in the poem, they maintain a faith that often sustains them far longer than their last job or warm meal. Is it simple necessity that forces poor people to trust God more than the rest of us?

My suspicion is that this urgency of needing food, shelter, and work combined with a lack of other self-controlled resources facilitates knowing God. In this session we'll explore this hypothesis, decide if Scripture bears it out or not, and see what we can learn about our own relationships with money by the way we regard the poor.

▼ ▼ ▼ ▼ ▼ ▼ ▼ ▼ ▼ ▼ ▼ ▼ ▼ ▼ ▼ ▼ ▼ ▼ ▼

Beginning   15 minutes

1. You pull up to a busy intersection with a long stoplight. On the highway's shoulder right next to you is an older man with dirty, unkempt clothes and a hand-scrawled cardboard sign reading: "Veteran will work for food. Kids at home sick. Please help. God bless." Which of the following best describes your typical reaction?

   ❒ You're uncomfortable and discreetly ignore the man until the light changes.

   ❒ You smile or nod at him, saying a prayer that the Lord will take care of him and meet his needs.

   ❒ You're annoyed and wonder if the man's a con-artist, duping sympathetic motorists for money to support a bad habit. You doubt that he's really a veteran or that there are sick children at home.

   ❒ You rummage in your purse or wallet for some money to hand him.

   ❒ You pull over, offer him a ride to a shelter or your church, give him some money and buy him a meal.

   ❒ You are moved to tears thinking about this man's plight and wonder why God allows some people to suffer more than others.

   ❒ You take him to your home and put him to work doing odd jobs around the house, paying him with both food and money.

   ❒ Other:

2. What words come to mind when you think of the word "poor"?

47

The Text
5 minutes

The following passage, taken from Jesus' Sermon on the Mount, is usually referred to as the Beatitudes because it describes people who are blessed. Pay attention to common denominators among those Jesus describes as blessed.

Have someone read the passages aloud. You may want to read the reference notes on pages 53-54 as well.

When Jesus saw his ministry drawing huge crowds, he climbed a hillside. Those who were apprenticed to him, the committed, climbed with him. Arriving at a quiet place, he sat down and taught his climbing companions. This is what he said:

"**You're blessed** when you're at the end of your rope. With less of you there is more of God and his rule.

"You're blessed when you feel you've lost what is most dear to you. Only then can you be embraced by the One most dear to you.

"You're blessed when you're content with just who you are—no more, no less. That's the moment you find yourselves proud owners of everything that can't be bought.

"You're blessed when you've worked up a good appetite for God. He's food and drink in the best meal you'll ever eat.

"You're blessed when you care. At the moment of being 'care-full,' you find yourselves cared for.

"You're blessed when you get your inside world— your mind and heart—put right. Then you can see God in the outside world.

"You're blessed when you can show people how to cooperate instead of compete or fight. That's when you discover who you really are, and your place in God's family.

"You're blessed when your commitment to God provokes persecution. The persecution drives you even deeper into God's kingdom.

"Not only that—count yourselves blessed every time people put you down or throw you out or speak lies about

48

you to discredit me. What it means is that the truth is too close for comfort and they are uncomfortable. You can be glad when that happens—give a cheer, even!—for though they don't like it, *I* do! And **all heaven applauds**. And know that you are in good company. My prophets and witnesses have always gotten into this kind of trouble."

(Matthew 5:1-12)

Understanding the Text   20 minutes

3. How would you define the word "blessed" based on what Jesus said?

4. Make a list or underline the traits of people who are blessed based on Jesus' observations here.

   a. What do they have in common?

   b. What kinds of attitudes do you think the blessed have toward money and wealth?

5. What effect does Jesus' repetition—"You're blessed when"—have on you when you read this passage?

6. Imagine what it must have been like to be in the crowd listening to Jesus. How do you think the people reacted to Jesus' words? Why?

▼ ▼ ▼ ▼ ▼ ▼ ▼ ▼ ▼ ▼ ▼ ▼ ▼ ▼ ▼ ▼ ▼ ▼ ▼
Applying the Text   20 minutes

7. a. Which one of the Beatitudes stands out to you the most? Why?

b. How does it relate to your attitude toward money?

8. While the first Beatitude is often translated as "Blessed are the poor in spirit," these verses don't necessarily apply to those who are materially poor. Nonetheless, many listeners then and many Christians today believe that these traits are often more apparent in the poor.

a. Do you think it's easier for poor people to trust God than for people who have more? Why, or why not?

b. Are there any "blessings" among the Beatitudes you think you would have if you were poorer? Which ones? Why?

9. Have you ever struggled financially? Think back to a time in your life when you were struggling financially. How would you describe that time in your life? Check as many as apply.

- ❒ I thought back on other, similar times and the way God had sustained me then.
- ❒ I panicked and worried myself silly about how the bills would be paid.
- ❒ I tried not to let anyone else know that I was in dire straits. It's embarrassing to struggle about money.
- ❒ I experienced unexpected gifts from family and friends and viewed it as God's provision.
- ❒ I charged and/or borrowed more money to survive then; in many ways I'm still in a tough spot paying for that time!
- ❒ I asked God for help then, but I struggle now to see how He helped me.
- ❒ I felt ashamed.
- ❒ I was annoyed and a little frustrated but knew it would pass.
- ❒ I grew closer to God during this time.
- ❒ Other:

10. Imagine that you'll wake up tomorrow and lose your job and all your savings without any warning.

a. How would you respond?

b. What fears would you have?

c. What plans would you make?

11. How does thinking about being suddenly impoverished make you feel?

- ❐ Scared. What can I do to prevent this from happening?
- ❐ Insecure. It's happened to others; it could happen to me, too.
- ❐ Doubtful. I don't think that would happen to me.
- ❐ Secure. I know that God would provide me with whatever I'd need.
- ❐ Other:

Assignment

Choose one of the following options to complete during the coming week.

1. Watch a film such as *Les Miserables, The Grapes of Wrath,* or *Titanic* and talk with other group members about how poor people are depicted in the film. How do the poor compare to their wealthy counterparts? How does the way they see the world differ? Which characters do you relate to most? Why?

2. Journal this week on the Beatitudes and your response to each one. With which ones do you struggle the most? Which ones seem to come easily? Choose one Beatitude and your response to share with the group next session.

3. Volunteer one hour of your time, either individually or corporately, to work in a homeless shelter, mission, or ministry to the poor. As quickly after the experience as possible, describe what took place. How did you feel being there? What kinds of people did you help or work with? Other than the constraints of time and your schedule, what keeps you from this kind of ministry more often?

▼ ▼ ▼ ▼ ▼ ▼ ▼ ▼ ▼ ▼ ▼ ▼ ▼ ▼ ▼ ▼ ▼ ▼ ▼ ▼
Prayer   10 minutes

Let each person complete this sentence: "Father, help me learn _____ from the Beatitudes so I might view money and material possessions the way You do." Pray for individual requests or needs. (If you prefer to pray silently, simply say "Amen" at your turn to signal the next person.)

▼ ▼ ▼ ▼ ▼ ▼ ▼ ▼ ▼ ▼ ▼ ▼ ▼ ▼ ▼ ▼ ▼ ▼ ▼ ▼
Reference Notes

Setting: As we noted back in session 2, one of Matthew's themes is to depict the contrast between the Jews' version of righteousness and Jesus' gift of grace. In this poetic, repetitive form, Jesus once again emphasizes that the truly righteous seek God more than the recognition of others. Many of the multitudes listening would be considered poor or working class along with a sprinkling of suspicious Pharisees and curious leaders.

You're blessed: The Greek word *makarios* is used here and usually translated as "blessed." However, that rendering does not fully capture the joy, wholeness, contentment, or peace that is intrinsic to the original language. Some scholars suggest that the Hebrew word *shalom*, "peace," comes closer. Regardless of how it's interpreted, the word clearly serves as the antithesis of the worried, harried, self-seeking, anxious people we see in many other passages (the rich young ruler, the certain rich man, the Pharisees, and others).

Note, too, that qualifications for blessedness all have to do with emptying ourselves and recognizing our weaknesses as opportunities to depend on and grow in our Father's love.

all heaven applauds: Once more, we see the contrast between what happens here on earth, from our limited points of view, and what happens when we store our treasures in heaven.

---

1. F. Scott Fitzgerald, *The Great Gatsby* (New York: Scribners, 1925), p. 184.
2. From the Institute for Research on Poverty (IRP) website: http://www.ssc.wisc.edu/irp/faq2.htm (February 20, 1998).
3. Untitled, unpublished poem by Tammy, a thirty-year-old woman at a mission for the homeless in Knoxville, Tennessee.

Tithes and Talents

▼ ▼ ▼ ▼ ▼ ▼ ▼ ▼ ▼ ▼ ▼ ▼ ▼ ▼ ▼ ▼ ▼ ▼ ▼

Overview   10 minutes

❶ *Welcome your group members. Compare homework assignments and ask someone to summarize last week's discussion. Then have someone read the following.*

I struggle with knowing when and how much money to give to my church, to missionary friends, to charities, to good causes like school libraries or drug intervention programs. I wrestle even more when money is tight, such as when the car breaks down or when Christmas presents cost more than budgeted. *Should I still give the same amount? Am I a terrible person if I skip a month's giving? Is my gift of five percent of that month's stretched income just as worthy as ten percent during a more relaxed month?*

Like most of us, I carry the baggage of conflicting messages about giving and stewardship. I grew up in a church that enforced the tithe: Christians must give at least ten percent of their gross income to the church before they budget anything else. This was justified by Leviticus 27:30-33, where Moses reports God's commands to the Israelites:

> "A tithe of everything from the land, whether grain from the soil or fruit from the trees, belongs to the LORD; it is holy to the LORD. If a man redeems any of his tithe, he must add a fifth of the value to it. The entire tithe of the

herd and flock—every tenth animal that passes under the shepherd's rod—will be holy to the LORD. He must not pick out the good from the bad or make any substitution. If he does make a substitution, both the animal and its substitute become holy and cannot be redeemed." (NIV)

Later in life, at a different church, I was told that Levitical Law no longer applied to modern believers because Jesus fulfilled the requirements of the Law and set believers free under the covenant of grace. I was told we should give as much as we're able and willing to give. Ten percent was regarded as a good guideline but not a legal obligation.

You may have similar views or variations of these. Even if issues of stewardship seem clear-cut to you, there are likely still times when you struggle with how to be a good steward in today's world.

In this session we will explore these tensions and look at what Jesus reveals about stewardship. Keep in mind we're not trying to derive a mathematical formula to calculate personal giving but an aspect of relationship to be experienced.

▼ ▼ ▼ ▼ ▼ ▼ ▼ ▼ ▼ ▼ ▼ ▼ ▼ ▼ ▼ ▼ ▼ ▼ ▼
Beginning   15 minutes

1. There are many words and phrases in the church that pertain to money. Take a moment to look at the words on the left. Respond with the first thing that comes to mind for each word. Don't worry about "right" answers, just jot down whatever comes to mind.

Word	Responses
Tithe	
Building program	
Poverty	
Stewardship	
Fundraising	

Wealth	
Charity	
Missions	
Budget	

2. a. Go around the room sharing each person's responses. Were responses similar or different for the members of your group?

   b. What did you learn about yourself based on your responses? About the group?

3. a. How have you been instructed in the past to give to the church? To charitable causes?

   b. Where did that instruction come from?

4. What criteria do you use when deciding how much and to whom you give?

▼ ▼ ▼ ▼ ▼ ▼ ▼ ▼ ▼ ▼ ▼ ▼ ▼ ▼ ▼ ▼ ▼ ▼ ▼

The Text   5 minutes

Have someone read the following passages out loud. You may
wish to read the reference notes on pages 63-64 as well.

> "[God's kingdom is] like **a man going off on an extended
> trip.** He called his servants together and delegated respon-
> sibilities. To one he gave **five thousand** dollars, to another
> **two thousand,** to a third **one thousand,** depending on
> their abilities. Then he left. Right off, the first servant went
> to work and doubled his master's investment. The second
> did the same. But the man with the single thousand dug a
> hole and carefully **buried his master's money.**
>
> "After a long absence, the master of those three ser-
> vants came back and settled up with them. The one given
> five thousand dollars showed him how he had doubled his
> investment. His master commended him: 'Good work! **You
> did your job well.** From now on be my partner.'
> "The servant with the two thousand showed how he
> also had doubled his master's investment. His master
> commended him: 'Good work! You did your job well. From
> now on be my partner.'
> "The servant given one thousand said, 'Master, I
> know you have high standards and hate careless ways, that
> you demand the best and make no allowances for error. **I
> was afraid** I might disappoint you, so I found a good hid-
> ing place and secured your money. Here it is, safe and
> sound down to the last cent.'
> "The master was furious. 'That's a terrible way to live!
> It's criminal to live cautiously like that! If you knew I was
> after the best, why did you do less than the least? The least
> you could have done would have been to invest the sum
> with the bankers, where at least I would have gotten a little
> interest.
> ""Take the thousand and give it to the one who risked
> the most. And get rid of this "play-it-safe" who won't go
> out on a limb. Throw him out into **utter darkness.**'"
>
> (Matthew 25:14-30)

Sitting across from the offering box, he was observing how the crowd tossed money in for the collection. Many of the rich were making large contributions. **One poor widow** came up and put in **two small coins**—a measly two cents. Jesus called his disciples over and said, "The truth is that this poor widow gave more to the collection than all the others put together. All the others gave what they'll never miss; she gave extravagantly what she couldn't afford—**she gave her all**." (Mark 12:41-43)

▼ ▼ ▼ ▼ ▼ ▼ ▼ ▼ ▼ ▼ ▼ ▼ ▼ ▼ ▼ ▼ ▼ ▼ ▼ ▼

Understanding the Text   15 minutes

5. a. In the first passage, how did the man decide how to delegate responsibility before he left on his trip?

   b. Do you think he left specific instructions with his servants? Why, or why not?

6. What do you think his expectations were regarding his affairs upon his return? Why?

7. a. The Bible doesn't say how the first two servants doubled their master's money. How much of a risk do you suppose they took?

b. How do you think the master would have responded to them had their risk been the same but they lost the investment?

8. What kinds of fears do you think kept the third servant from action?

9. Why was the man so harsh with the third servant? (After all, he didn't lose any money!)

10. a. Why did Jesus respond the way He did to the widow in the second passage?

b. Discuss the difference between bold risk-taking and foolhardy abandon. Under what circumstances might Jesus have praised the widow for holding onto her two cents?

▼ ▼ ▼ ▼ ▼ ▼ ▼ ▼ ▼ ▼ ▼ ▼ ▼ ▼ ▼ ▼ ▼ ▼ ▼

Applying the Text   15 minutes

11. a. Reread the story of the man and his servants. Which character do you identify with most? Why?

b. In general, is it easier for you to take risks or to think of the things that might go wrong?

12. What kinds of resources and responsibilities do you think God has given you? What has happened in your life to affirm that belief?

13. a. As you think of those things, are you capitalizing on them or hiding them? Is there an example you can share with the group?

   b. What are some new ways you can use those resources or abilities for God?

14. Have you ever felt like the widow in the second passage? If so, describe when and why.

15. Have you ever made a sacrifice that seemed "measly" to others but big to you? What was the result?

16. Some people would argue that this passage is telling believers to give up all they have. How do you respond to that argument?

Assignment

Read the following case study and journal your responses to the questions that follow.

> Your church discovers a surplus of funds at the end of the year. The leadership team, along with the church's accountant, narrows the choices of how to spend the money down to three. The church could (1) increase annual giving to a family in the church who recently became missionaries in Slovenia; (2) replace the roof over the sanctuary because it has a small leak in the back corner; or (3) place it in the deacon's fund for poor people, emergencies, and food banks.
>
> Since your group has been focusing on money, the leaders ask you to speak on behalf of the group and answer the following questions:

1. Which option would you choose? Why?

2. What would you encourage the leadership to keep in mind as they decided what to do with the money?

3. How do the passages from this lesson influence your decision?

Prayer   10 minutes

Let each member share at least one area where he or she would like to be a better steward, being as specific as is comfortable. Remain seated and spend a minute or two in silent prayer. Then whoever would like to pray may do so. After everyone has had an opportunity, the leader should close.

▼ ▼

Reference Notes

Settings: In the passage from Matthew, Jesus' disciples have gathered around Him privately on the Mount of Olives to inquire about His death, resurrection, and second coming (Matthew 24:1-3). They were getting nervous about the growing antagonism between the Pharisees and Jesus, especially as their Master continued to expose the religious leaders' hypocrisy and selfishness (Matthew 23). Jesus responds by describing the peril at hand (24:15-31) and by telling several parables (about the fig tree and ten virgins), including this one about the talents.

Mark's gospel focuses on Jesus as the Servant of God. This is reinforced by even the small stories, including the one where Christ recognizes the immense sacrifice of the widow's offering.

a man going off on an extended trip: Jesus describes Himself as the master delegating his kingdom to his servants, pointing to the role of diligence, singular focus, and preparation in the life of believers.

five thousand, two thousand, one thousand: The common translation for each of these is "talent," which was not a denomination of currency but a weight, roughly equivalent to twenty-five kilograms of gold or silver. The interpretation of these goods left by the master as spiritual gifts can be drawn metaphorically but not literally. However, the principle that we should risk using what we have been entrusted with holds true for personal as well as material resources.

buried his master's money: A common practice among the Jewish who did not have banks or safe-deposit boxes was to bury valuables in an inconspicuous field. This compares to "hiding our light under a bushel" (Matthew 5:15).

You did your job well: The praise of the master carries with it increased responsibility. We are entrusted with more when we prove faithful.

I was afraid: The third steward sought to blame and excuse his behavior. Notice that he claimed to know his master's character

("I know you have high standards and hate careless ways") but not thoroughly enough (The master says, "What a terrible way to live!"). Too often our fears—loss of affirmation, power, identity, or comfort—keep us from using what we've been given for God's kingdom.

utter darkness: While the consequences may seem harsh, they are natural consequences of placing self before God. When we neglect opportunities, the penalty is often the loss of further opportunities. This reference to "utter darkness" parallels what the steward did with the money itself: he buried it in dormancy. This seems to reinforce further that how we live as stewards reflects our faith and our ultimate treasure in heaven.

Sitting across from the offering box: Jesus watched in front of the Temple "treasury," which contained thirteen trumpet-shaped chests for various offerings, each marked for different purposes—incense, sacrifices, wood, and so on. While He saw the rich give many offerings, Christ was not impressed because He could see into the heart of each giver. Also, the wealthy tended to make a large ceremonious display of how much they were dropping in each coffer.

One poor widow: The equal emphasis on "one" and "poor" implies loneliness as well as poverty. She was both emotionally and financially bereft.

two small coins: The widow gives two coins, *lepta*, which were small, copper, penny-like disks. While it's nearly impossible to equate to today's market value, the coins were each worth about one-fifth of a penny then. Her offering was considered insulting by the Pharisees and wealthy congregants; however, Jesus saw that it was everything she had. It's interesting, too, that she likely would be justified in not giving because of her poverty, but she gave freely nonetheless.

she gave her all: Once more, we see that it's not so much our money that God wants; it's us. But how we relate to money and our willingness to use it for His kingdom purposes tends to reflect how much of us belongs to Him.

Plastic Paradise

▼ ▼ ▼ ▼ ▼ ▼ ▼ ▼ ▼ ▼ ▼ ▼ ▼ ▼ ▼ ▼ ▼ ▼ ▼ ▼

Overview   5 minutes

❶ *Welcome group members. Discuss the homework assign-ment and have someone recap the discussion from last session. Then have someone read the following.*

Congratulations! You've been pre-approved for up to $50,000 in a line of credit from Pilgrimage Growth Guide Bank. You are one of a select few[1] who have demonstrated the financial credentials necessary to carry the new Pilgrimage Platinum Charge Card. As such, you will be especially interested in the prestigious benefits this card can provide to those who've earned this invitation.

Your privileges include having the purchasing power to take charge of your life—you can travel, shop, or transfer bal-ances from other cards with the security of knowing that you're paying one of the lowest interest rates around.[2] No other card compares for value, flexibility, and savings. As an added reward, we'll be sending you a special gift befitting a Platinum Cardholder such as yourself. Just use your card to make a pur-chase or balance transfer of at least $500 within one month of receiving your card—it's that simple!

Sound familiar? If your home is like mine, you receive numerous "pre-approved invitations" each week urging you to open a new credit card account. That's in addition to bills, infor-mation, and promotions sent by the credit card companies we already do business with. According to recent articles in *Forbes* and *Money* magazines, the average American now carries nine credit cards with a combined balance of about $1,600. (Remember that average includes people who pay off their balances every month as well as those who carry balances of tens of thousands of dollars.)[3] In 1996, a record 1.1 million Americans filed for personal bankruptcy, up twenty-nine percent from 1995, sticking credit card issuers for $8.1 billion dollars in losses.[4]

While I haven't considered bankruptcy, I'll admit I don't like the way I've used credit in the past to purchase family vacations, emergency auto repairs, or splurges to make me feel better. I want to manage our family's finances in a more responsible, God-honoring way and resist the idolatry of consumption that encourages people to go deeper into debt instead of freeing up more resources for God's kingdom.

This process has produced several difficult questions along the way: How does God view debt? Are some debts okay and others not? If so, how do I tell the difference? What does my use of credit reveal about my relationship with money? With God?

In this session we'll explore these questions as we think about the role debt plays in the process of becoming good stewards.

▼ ▼

Beginning   15 minutes

1. How was debt viewed in the family you grew up in? How did that affect your family's finances?

2. Before the discussion continues, it would be helpful to define debt. How would you describe it? (Check all that apply.)
   ❏ Credit cards
   ❏ Student loans
   ❏ House payments
   ❏ Car payments
   ❏ Loans
   ❏ Other:

3. What's your usual response to the kind of credit offer extended above (created as a composite from actual credit solicitations)?

4. a. When did you get your first credit card? How did it make you feel?

   b. Do you still carry it? How do you feel about it now?

5. How would you feel if the other group members were informed of the amount of debt you're in right now? Check as many of the following as apply.

   ❏ A little awkward, but okay as long as I got to see their debts too.
   ❏ Terrified! I'd be totally humiliated and embarrassed.
   ❏ Proud of the way I discipline myself and my family's finances.
   ❏ Ashamed of myself. Can a real Christian really be this irresponsible with money?
   ❏ Humbled by others' recognition of how much I live above my means.
   ❏ Annoyed. It's really none of their business.
   ❏ Not great, but okay. I'm in debt, but so is everyone else, right? It could be a lot worse.
   ❏ Great! I'm not in debt right now.
   ❏ Other:

The Text   5 minutes

Deuteronomy is largely a book collecting and explaining the fine points of various Jewish laws; the word itself means "a second copy of the law." In the first passage below we see how God instructed the Israelites to handle debt.

Following that passage is Paul's instruction to Christians at Rome, where the diverse group (Jewish, Gentile, rich and poor believers) found themselves struggling to know whether to abide by the capital empire's laws.

❶ *Have someone read aloud the following passages. You may want to read the reference notes on pages 74-76.*

At the end of **every seven years** you must cancel debts. This is how it is to be done: Every creditor shall **cancel the loan** he has made to his fellow Israelite. He shall not require payment from his fellow Israelite or brother, because the LORD's time for canceling debts has been proclaimed. You may require payment from a foreigner, but you must cancel any debt your brother owes you. However, there should be no poor among you, for in the land the LORD your God is giving you to possess as your inheritance, he will richly bless you, if only you fully obey the LORD your God and are careful to follow all these commands I am giving you today. For the LORD your God will bless you as he has promised, and **you will lend to many nations but will borrow from none**. You will rule over many nations but none will rule over you.

(Deuteronomy 15:1-6, NIV)

Be a good citizen. **All governments are under God.** Insofar as there is peace and order, it's God's order. So live responsibly as a citizen. If you're irresponsible to the state, then you're irresponsible with God, and God will hold you responsible. Duly constituted authorities are only a threat if you're trying to get by with something. Decent citizens should have nothing to fear.

Do you want to be on good terms with the government? Be a responsible citizen and you'll get on just fine, the government working to your advantage. But if you're breaking the rules right and left, watch out. The police aren't there just to be admired in their uniforms. God also has an interest in keeping order, and he uses them to do it. That's why you must live responsibly—not just to avoid punishment but also because it's the right way to live.

That's also why you pay taxes—so that an orderly way of life can be maintained. Fulfill your obligations as a citizen. Pay your taxes, pay your bills, respect your leaders.

Don't run up debts, except for the huge debt of love you owe each other.

(Romans 13:1-8)

▼ ▼ ▼ ▼ ▼ ▼ ▼ ▼ ▼ ▼ ▼ ▼ ▼ ▼ ▼ ▼ ▼ ▼ ▼ ▼
Understanding the Text   15 minutes

6. a. What's the principle behind canceling debts every seven years?

b. How did this practice strengthen the Israelites' relationship with God? With each other?

7. Why do you suppose the Israelites could require payment from foreigners but not each other at the end of seven years?

8. a. Why should there be "no poor among you"?

b. Do you think this was a goal to aim for or a reality for the Israelites to whom this passage was written? Why?

9. a. What was Paul's basic argument in this section of his letter to the Romans?

b. On what did he base his argument?

10. Why do you think Paul addressed debt within the context of being a good citizen?

11. a. Why shouldn't believers run up debts? What reasons do you think are behind this strong command?

b. Does this same assumption hold true today or have changing times and economies altered Paul's point?

12. What do you think Paul means by "the huge debt of love that you owe each other"?

▼ ▼ ▼ ▼ ▼ ▼ ▼ ▼ ▼ ▼ ▼ ▼ ▼ ▼ ▼ ▼ ▼ ▼ ▼ ▼
Applying the Text   15 minutes

13. a. Do you think the principle behind canceling debt every
       seven years would work in our current economy? Why, or
       why not?

    b. Would you want to participate if it were practiced today?
       Why, or why not?

14. Do you think Paul would carry a credit card today? Why, or
    why not? (You may want to refer to Acts 17 as well as the
    passage from this session.)

15. a. Are there times when it's appropriate to go into debt?
       Make a list of situations you think merit debt and show
       responsible stewardship. Keep a separate list of situations
       where you think debt would display poor stewardship.

    b. Are there clear boundaries between your lists or is it an
       individual matter between a person and God? How do you
       decide?

16. Read the following case study and then answer the questions that follow.

Alice and Jerry have been married for fifteen years and have three children, ages 8, 11, and 12. They thought they would be getting a large tax refund in April and made plans to take the entire family to Disney World in May. The kids were thrilled. But then they discovered an error on their forms. Rather than receiving a sizable refund, they ended up having to pay a small amount of income tax.

Nonetheless, Jerry wants to use the couple's credit cards to fund the vacation. Alice is against the idea since they still owe a few hundred dollars from their purchases at Christmas. Jerry argues, "But this is a once-in-a-lifetime trip. We can't disappoint the kids."

a. Jerry and Alice come to you for advice. What would you advise them to do? Why?

b. Do you agree with Jerry's logic that this is a once-in-a-life-time trip that justifies going into debt?

c. Do any events—getting married, a tenth anniversary, a fortieth birthday—justify splurging even if it means going in debt? Why, or why not?

▼ ▼ ▼ ▼ ▼ ▼ ▼ ▼ ▼ ▼ ▼ ▼ ▼ ▼ ▼ ▼ ▼ ▼ ▼

Assignment   5 minutes

Choose one of the following options to complete before next session.

1. In your journal complete the following statements:

   ❐ Honestly, I feel _____ when I think about

   my situation with debt.

   ❐ Credit cards should only be used when

   _____,

   although I tend to use them when

   _____.

   ❐ Responsible use of debt includes:

   _____.

2. If you were debt-free, how would your relationship with God be different? Generally, would it be easier or harder to depend on God? Why? (If you don't have debt, complete this statement: Because I am debt-free, my relationship with God is. . . .) Record your answer in your journal.

3. Choose one of the books from the **Additional Resources** section on page 76 and begin reading it. You may decide to read and discuss it with other group members, even after the group switches topics or stops meeting. Or, you may want to read it for yourself and journal your responses. In either case, set at least one debt-related goal for the next year.

❶ *Ask if any group members are knowledgeable and/or gifted in financial planning. If so, schedule a meeting soon where group members can bring questions about budgets, getting out of debt, retirement funds, and shopping habits. If no one in the group feels qualified, seek out someone in the church at large who might be willing to host such a meeting (perhaps at a reduced fee).*

▼ ▼

Prayer   5 minutes

Let each person share at least one area of financial concern that they'd like to pray for. Then pray for each other by name. As usual, if you'd rather pray silently, just say "Amen" to signal the next person that you're done.

▼ ▼ ▼ ▼ ▼ ▼ ▼ ▼ ▼ ▼ ▼ ▼ ▼ ▼ ▼ ▼ ▼ ▼ ▼ ▼

Reference Notes

Settings: While most of us don't consider Deuteronomy our favorite Old Testament book, it was well-known among the Jews as one of the fundamental books on God's law. The book's themes emerge clearly: to remember God's goodness, to obey His laws out of loving loyalty, and to behold what He has in store for His people. This passage embodies all three of these themes as did the holiday it reflects, the Year of Jubilee, a time of commemoration, celebration, and anticipation.

In Paul's letter to the Christians in Rome, he addresses a major source of contention among the mixed group (Jewish and Gentile believers along with Roman converts). They apparently disagreed over whether to obey the Roman laws, especially tax laws, when they felt more allegiance to God as their ultimate ruler. After all, money paid for taxes could be financing other church and missions endeavors. However, as we see here, Paul clearly instructs them that honoring authority does honor God.

every seven years: The seventh year was called the Sabbatic Year and was celebrated by the Israelites as a reminder of God's goodness and mercy to them. It also reinforced the lesson of creation—even Yahweh rested on the Sabbath after creating on the previous six days. The emphasis during the Sabbatic Year was to show each other the same mercy that God had shown them collectively. The sabbatical year is still practiced in some professions, especially academia, where a professor may be given the seventh year to write, read, and research rather than to teach and administrate.

cancel the loan: Many scholars debate whether this meant that the loan was postponed for a year's time or whether it was canceled completely. Most seemed to think that debts were merely suspended for the Sabbatic Year and then collected afterward. Only in the Year of Jubilee (every fiftieth year—see Leviticus 25) would all debts actually be canceled, interpret these scholars.

you will lend to many nations but will borrow from none: This prophetic commandment reflects the variable of power possessed by a lender of money. We see this echoed in the Scriptures ("The rich rule over the poor, and the borrower is servant to the lender," Proverbs 22:7, NIV), in literature (Shakespeare's *The Merchant of Venice*), and in history (consider the feudal system of the Middle Ages or even our own stock market crash of 1929). This seems very logical—if you owe someone money, that person holds power over you.

All governments are under God: Amidst the sharp rising and falling of the Roman Republic and then Empire, Paul reminded his fellow believers in the Roman Church that God's sovereignty reigned amidst the long stretches of peace (the reigns of Seneca, Burrus, and the first five years of Nero), or the sudden tumultuous upheavals (the tragic chaos of A.D. 66). These wise words are repeated in other letters to believers at other locales— 1 Timothy 2, Titus 3:1, and echoed in 1 Peter 3:13-17. Paul was fully aware that the Christian church, including the mixed group at Rome, could no longer be recognized as solely a Jewish entity. Consequently, Christians had no recognized political standing.

Don't run up debts: Paul summed up his double message to the church—be good representatives of Christ by obeying the government, and forget old grudges by loving each other well— in this simple phrase. This message connects back to the principle behind the Sabbatic Year, that we cancel our debts toward one another (Jesus and Paul would say everyone, not just our fellow ethnic brothers and sisters) because of the unpayable debt of gratitude that we have to the Father.

▼ ▼ ▼ ▼ ▼ ▼ ▼ ▼ ▼ ▼ ▼ ▼ ▼ ▼ ▼ ▼ ▼ ▼ ▼ ▼

Additional Resources

The Money Diet: Reaping the Rewards of Financial Fitness, Ginger Applegarth (New York: Penguin, 1996).

How to Get Out of Debt, Stay Out of Debt, and Live Prosperously, Jerrold Mundis (New York: Bantam, 1994).

The Secret Meaning of Money: How It Binds Together Families in Love, Envy, Compassion, or Anger, Cloe Madanes with Claudio Madanes (New York: Jossey-Bass, 1996).

The Millionaire Next Door: The Surprising Secrets of America's Wealthy, Thomas J. Stanley and William D. Danko (Atlanta: Longstreet, 1996).

---

1. Credit card companies mailed out 7.5 *billion* credit offers between 1994 and 1996, the majority pre-approved according to Janet Novack, "Debtors' Vision," *Forbes,* June 2, 1997, pp. 45-46.
2. At the time this was written, the annual percentage rate (APR) average for credit cards, excluding introductory "teaser" rates which only last for three to six months, was 17.9 percent.
3. Peter Keating, "How to Avoid Being Swamped by Your Credit-Card Debt," *Money,* March 1995, p. 40.
4. Novack, p. 45.

Saving

▼ ▼ ▼ ▼ ▼ ▼ ▼ ▼ ▼ ▼ ▼ ▼ ▼ ▼ ▼ ▼ ▼ ▼ ▼
Overview   10 minutes

❶ *Greet the group members. Since this is the next-to-last session, ask group members to decide by next time whether they would like to continue in the group or not and whether to stick with the same topic or switch to another. If time permits, ask someone to sum up the discussion from last time. Then have someone else read the following.*

In the film *It's a Wonderful Life*, Jimmy Stewart's character George Bailey inherits his father's savings and loan business, as well as his passion for providing townspeople a reasonable choice besides the villainous Mr. Potter. One of my favorite scenes is when George and Mary are about to leave for their honeymoon and there's a run on the bank due to the stock market crash. As customers clamor for their funds, George tries to explain the way a savings and loan operates. He tells one man that his savings are invested in someone else's home mortgage and another woman that her nest egg is tied up in a small business loan. George stresses the notion of community and personal sacrifice to help everyone survive the desperate times. The people retort that it's their money and they're entitled to what they've saved—if ever there's a good time to withdraw it, it seems like now. As you probably recall, it isn't easy, but George manages to keep his customers, and his company, in business.

That scene was one of the first I can recall that helped me

make any sense out of how banks operated. As a child I wondered how they could survive if they were giving out loans all the time and what happened to my handful of dollars that I deposited in my meager savings account each year after my birthday and Christmas. While saving money does not come naturally to me, I've learned to view it as a large part of the stewardship to which God calls us. I've also learned what it means to spend what I've saved at His prompting. Both experiences require discipline. But being a steward who saves resources to use in the future also requires vision, generosity, and trust in God's timing.

In this session we will examine these traits, as well as our attitudes toward saving, to see what's involved in being better savers and stewards of our financial resources.

▼ ▼
Beginning   15 minutes

1. When you were a child, did you spend all of your birthday money, some of it, or none of it? Why?

2. On a scale of 1 to 5 (1 being easy and 5 being difficult), how hard is it for you to save money?

1	2	3	4	5
easy				difficult

3. You have $10,000 in your savings account. Which of the following would be good causes for spending it?
   - ❏ Your daughter's wedding
   - ❏ Loaning it to your best friend who's lost her job
   - ❏ Living expenses and bills after being fired from your job
   - ❏ Living expenses and bills after quitting your job
   - ❏ An exotic week-long cruise for your twentieth wedding anniversary

- ❏ A short-term mission project to Eastern Europe
- ❏ Medical operation to remove your inflamed appendix
- ❏ Plastic surgery to remove your double chin
- ❏ New building program at your church
- ❏ Your child's first year of college tuition
- ❏ Other:

▼ ▼ ▼ ▼ ▼ ▼ ▼ ▼ ▼ ▼ ▼ ▼ ▼ ▼ ▼ ▼ ▼ ▼ ▼
The Text   5 minutes

Joseph lived a life of unparalleled peaks and valleys. He was betrayed by his brothers, sold into slavery, displaced in a foreign culture, almost seduced by a scheming wife, and imprisoned for a crime he didn't commit. Two years later the tide turned as God's faithfulness emerged clearly in the story. When Pharaoh had a confusing dream he searched for someone to interpret it. Joseph's former cellmate, the court butler, recalled how Joseph interpreted his own dream and told Pharaoh about Joseph.

❶ *Have someone read aloud the following passages. You may want to read the reference notes on pages 84-85.*

> So Pharaoh sent for Joseph, and he was quickly brought from the dungeon. When he had **shaved and changed** his clothes, he came before Pharaoh.
>
> Pharaoh said to Joseph, "I had a dream, and **no one can interpret it**. But I have heard it said of you that when you hear a dream you can interpret it."
>
> "**I cannot do it**," Joseph replied to Pharaoh, "but God will give Pharaoh the answer he desires."
>
> Then Pharaoh said to Joseph, "In my dream I was standing on the bank of the Nile, when out of the river there came up seven **cows**, fat and sleek, and they grazed among the reeds. After them, seven other cows came up— scrawny and very ugly and lean. I had never seen such ugly cows in all the land of Egypt. The lean, ugly cows ate up the seven fat cows that came up first. But even after they ate them, no one could tell that they had done so; they

looked just as ugly as before. Then I woke up.

"In my dreams I also saw seven **heads of grain**, full and good, growing on a single stalk. After them, seven other heads sprouted—withered and thin and scorched by the east wind. The thin heads of grain swallowed up the seven good heads. I told this to the magicians, but none could explain it to me."

Then Joseph said to Pharaoh, "The dreams of Pharaoh are one and the same. God has revealed to Pharaoh what he is about to do. The seven good cows are seven years, and the seven good heads of grain are seven years; it is one and the same dream. The seven lean, ugly cows that came up afterward are seven years, and so are the seven worthless heads of grain scorched by the east wind: They are seven years of famine.

"It is just as I said to Pharaoh: God has shown Pharaoh what he is about to do. Seven years of great abundance are coming throughout the land of Egypt, but seven years of famine will follow them. Then all the abundance in Egypt will be forgotten, and the famine will ravage the land. The abundance in the land will not be remembered, because the famine that follows it will be so severe. The reason the dream was given to Pharaoh in two forms is that the matter has been firmly decided by God, and God will do it soon.

"And now let Pharaoh look for **a discerning and wise man** and put him in charge of the land of Egypt. Let Pharaoh appoint commissioners over the land to take a fifth of the harvest of Egypt during the seven years of abundance. They should collect all the food of these good years that are coming and store up the grain under the authority of Pharaoh, to be kept in the cities for food. This food should be held in reserve for the country, to be used during the seven years of famine that will come upon Egypt, so that the country may not be ruined by the famine."

The plan seemed good to Pharaoh and to all his officials. So Pharaoh asked them, "Can we find anyone like this man, one in whom is the spirit of God?"

Then Pharaoh said to Joseph, "**Since God has made all this known to you**, there is no one so discerning and wise as you. You shall be in charge of my palace, and all my people are to submit to your orders. Only with respect to the throne will I be greater than you."

(Genesis 41:14-40, NIV)

80

Understanding the Text   15 minutes

4. Why do you think God sent His message to Pharaoh in dreams?

5. What was Joseph's role in God's plan?

6. What role do vision and foresight play in this passage?

7. Why do you think God would allow famine—especially since He warned Pharaoh first?

8. What leadership or stewardship qualifications did Joseph and Pharaoh display?

Applying the Text   15 minutes

9. God doesn't always warn us before we face a "famine" in our lives. Why do you think He allows us to go through financial hardship without warning?

10. In what ways can saving go against God's admonition not to "hoard treasure" as we saw in session 2?

11. Describe a time when you saved for a "lean, ugly cow" season. If you never have, imagine what your response would be.
   a. How did it feel as you tried to prepare in advance?

   b. How did you know when it was time to spend what you'd saved?

   c. How did it feel when you spent your savings?

12. Joseph instructed Pharaoh to put aside one-fifth of the plentiful harvests for the coming famine. Ideally, how much of your income do you think God calls you to save? Why?

13. a. Are you saving as much as you'd like? Too much? Not enough?

   b. How can you involve God in your saving?

Assignment 5 minutes

During the next week pray and journal about your commitment to the group, especially what you've enjoyed and benefited from and what you think needs improvement. Come to the next session prepared to offer feedback and share your suggestions for the group's direction.

Choose one of the following options to begin between now and the next session.

1. Journal your responses to the following:

   ❒ I need to save more for _____ and

   spend less on _____.

   ❒ I agree that saving money is a great principle, but the

   thing that gets me is _____.

   ❒ I plan on saving more money once

   _____ happens.

   ❒ For me, saving money is _____

   because _____.

2. If you have a savings account, pray and journal about whether God might be calling you to spend it for His kingdom causes, whether it's a personal need or a clear need of the church. Plan to call at least one other group member during the week and discuss what you feel the Holy Spirit is prompting you to do.

Prayer   5 minutes

Let each person share something he or she wishes to save for.
Pray for each other by name. Pray for the Holy Spirit's guidance
for the group as you each decide what direction to take next.

Reference Notes

Setting: One of the purposes of Genesis is to illustrate how
God and His people interact together. Of special significance is
the way God makes covenants, or committed promises, to His
people and their successors. Thus, we follow the generations
of famous families like Adam, Noah, Isaac, and Jacob. As we
see in this story of Joseph, God's loving faithfulness—His
ability to redeem human frailty, fear, and selfishness—
emerges consistently.

shaved and changed: While it would be natural for a dirty pris-
oner to bathe and change clothes before going to Pharaoh's
court, shaving would not be expected of a Hebrew who often
prided himself on his different appearance. This detail in the
story reinforces Joseph's willingness to serve God by relinquish-
ing any Jewish pride and fully integrated himself into Egyptian
society.

no one can interpret it; I cannot do it: Both phrases emphasize the unique dilemma of interpreting Pharaoh's dream—it
deals with the supernatural realm of God, not with logic
(although Joseph's rendering of it does clearly make sense) or
skill. Joseph's response that "I cannot do it, but God can" is similar to what he told the baker and the butler back in prison when
he helped them understand their dreams as well (Genesis
40:1-18). His calm humility contrasts with Pharaoh's distress
that none of his magicians, advisors, or seers could figure out
the dream.

cows, heads of grain: Both of these items continue to symbolize food supplies around the world today.

a discerning and wise man: Joseph may or may not have had himself in mind for the job. While many of us might have seen this as a perfect opportunity to negotiate freedom with Pharaoh, Joseph left this open to God's will as well. He didn't say, "My God insists that I fulfill this important role." Joseph's grace under pressure displays his fearless trust in his Lord.

Since God has made all this known to you: Pharaoh preceded this with the rhetorical question, "Where can we find anyone like this?" but then quickly realized his answer stood before him. It's remarkable that the leader of a nation of thousands, who all worshiped numerous gods, would recognize God's intervention and appoint a godly man as his second-in-command. It may seem like a stretch of the text, but in many ways how we live as stewards directly affects how unbelievers view God.

Freedom in Christ

▼ ▼

Overview   10 minutes

❶ *Invite group members to share what they learned from
the homework or what they've reflected on from the last
session's discussion. After five to ten minutes of discussion,
have someone read the following.*

In his book *Money, Sex, and Power*, Richard J. Foster shares the
following story:

> The lovable (and sometimes frustrating) Franciscan
> Brother Juniper had so learned the meaning of detachment
> [from money] that many thought he was a fool. On one
> occasion he came across an elaborate altar that had silver
> ringlets hanging from the frontal. He took one look at
> them and announced, "These ringlets are superfluous,"
> and proceeded to cut them off and give them to the poor.
> The village priest, of course, was outraged. Poor Juniper
> simply could not understand the priest's anger, for he
> assumed he had done him a great service by freeing him
> from the "display of worldly vanity." Saint Francis was so
> moved by the spirit of detachment he saw in Brother
> Juniper that on one occasion he cried out, "My brothers, if
> only I had a great forest of such junipers!"[1]

I'm guessing most of us don't share Brother Juniper's tendency to give away the church fixtures. If my own experience is

any example, then we struggle much more with "affluenza," the term coined for the diseased cycle of wanting, spending, and possessing. As we head into the twenty-first century, more and more socioeconomic research points to the disparity between Third World poverty and First World affluence.

Many Christians (and nonChristians, too, although for different reasons) have been deliberately downscaling during the last couple of decades. This is not an attempt to be super-spiritual through spartan living (often called *asceticism*), but an attempt to be better stewards — to walk between the extremes of selfish indulgence and selfless indifference.

During the past year and a half, my wife and I have been trying to rethink our finances, our credit card debt, and the ways and reasons we spend money. Our attempt at more purposeful stewardship has included hiring a friend who does financial consulting, taking out life insurance and making our wills, paying off and canceling as many credit cards as possible. This year we realized we struggle with impulse buying — especially things like clothes, books, and CDs. After cleaning our closets, we knew that we had plenty of nice clothes for almost all occasions. So, back in January we decided that we'd pick two calendar days — one spring, one fall — to shop for clothing. If we saw or thought of something we needed, then we added it to our spring or fall list. For books and music, we use the library more, trade magazines with friends, and request desired titles on birthday and Christmas lists.

None of these strategies may work for you. Or a few of them might. The key is to pursue God first and allow stewardship to emerge out of our loving relationship with Him. As John Calvin put it, "The only right stewardship is that which is tested by the rule of love."[2] This is the freedom we experience in Christ, trusting our Father to meet our deepest soul needs as well as the needs of the day. Out of such a relationship we are attuned to what it means to live for His kingdom — sometimes saving, sometimes spending, always giving.

Beginning   15 minutes

1. How have your views of money changed since this group began? What's made the difference?

2. What's one post-group financial goal you have for yourself?

3. a. Do you tend to be more like Brother Juniper or more like someone with affluenza?

   b. Why do both extremes tend to draw us away from good stewardship?

The Text   5 minutes

❶ *Have someone read aloud the following. You may also want to read the reference notes on pages 95-96.*

Jesus began a sermon before a crowd so large that they were stepping on each other (Luke 12:1) when a person from the crowd calls out, "Teacher, tell my brother to divide the family inheritance with me" (verse 13). Whether the person questioning Jesus was appealing to Jesus' knowledge of the Law or testing His knowledge of it we don't know. But ultimately this is not as important as the true motive behind the question. Jesus proceeded to warn against greed by telling the following parable.

Then he told them this story: "The farm of a certain rich man produced a terrific crop. He talked to himself: 'What can I do? My barn isn't big enough for this harvest.' Then he said, 'Here's what I'll do: I'll tear down my barns and build bigger ones. Then I'll gather in all my grain and goods, and I'll say to myself, "**Self**, you've done well! You've got it made and can now retire. Take it easy and have the time of your life!"'

"Just then God showed up and said, '**Fool**! Tonight you die. And your barnful of goods—who gets it?'

"That's what happens when you fill your barn with Self and not with God."

He continued **this subject** with his disciples. "Don't fuss about what's on the table at mealtimes or if the clothes in your closet are in fashion. There is far more to your inner life than the food you put in your stomach, more to your outer appearance than the clothes you hang on your body. Look at the **ravens**, free and unfettered, not tied down to a job description, carefree in the care of God. And you count far more.

"Has anyone by fussing before the mirror ever gotten taller by so much as an inch? If fussing can't even do that, why fuss at all? Walk into the fields and look at the wild-flowers. They don't fuss with their appearance—but have you ever seen color and design quite like it? The ten best-dressed men and women in the country look shabby alongside them. If God gives such attention to the wild-flowers, most of them never even seen, don't you think he'll attend to you, take pride in you, do his best for you?

"What I'm trying to do here is get you to **relax**, not be so **preoccupied** with *getting* so you can respond to God's *giving*. People who don't know God and the way he works fuss over these things, but you know both God and how he works. Steep yourself in God-reality, God-initiative, God-provisions. You'll find all your everyday human concerns will be met. Don't be afraid of missing out. You're my dearest friends! The Father wants to give you the very kingdom itself.

"Be generous. Give to the poor. Get yourselves a bank that can't go bankrupt, a bank in heaven far from

bankrobbers, safe from embezzlers, a bank you can bank
on. It's obvious, isn't it? The place where your treasure is,
is the place you will most want to be, and end up being."

(Luke 12:16-34)

Understanding the Text   15 minutes

4. a. What does the rich man in Jesus' story have in common
with the rich young ruler in session 3?

b. With the foolish steward in session 5?

5. Why was the rich man condemned for saving while people
like Joseph and Pharaoh were praised?

6. Notice what the rich man said to himself. What does wealth
mean to him?

7. What do think Jesus meant when He said there is far more
to our inner lives than just the food we eat or clothes we
wear?

8. a. Make a list of the reasons Jesus told His disciples to "be anxious for nothing."

   b. Why do you suppose Jesus used so many illustrations from nature to make His point?

9. How does worry make you "preoccupied with getting"?

▼ ▼ ▼ ▼ ▼ ▼ ▼ ▼ ▼ ▼ ▼ ▼ ▼ ▼ ▼ ▼ ▼ ▼ ▼ ▼

Applying the Text   15 minutes

10. a. According to Jesus' words, how can we become free from the power money holds over so many people?

    b. What would the kind of freedom Jesus described look like in your life? What would need to change?

11. Why did Jesus stress "earthly" reasons (reducing anxiety, not being robbed or embezzled, not going bankrupt, and so on) to bank in heaven as opposed to more spiritual ones?

12. Jesus commanded us to be generous. Have you ever found freedom in an act of generosity? If so, share it with the group.

13. Think of at least one money-related concern, perhaps one you've been praying about with the group. How does this passage help you discern the significance of your concern?

14. a. What's one area as God's steward where you need more balance?

b. How will you pursue this balance? Set at least one post-group goal for yourself to fulfill this pursuit of balanced stewardship. It might be reading a book, meeting with a financial planner, asking someone you trust for help, or giving more.

▼ ▼ ▼ ▼ ▼ ▼ ▼ ▼ ▼ ▼ ▼ ▼ ▼ ▼ ▼ ▼ ▼ ▼ ▼
Assignment   5 minutes

Choose one of the following options:

1. Spend some time in your journal thinking through your original hopes and expectations for this group. Which ones have been met? In what ways are you disappointed? What

was the best aspect of the group? What area most needed to be done differently? How do you view money differently from when you started the group? Will you treat money any differently from before the group? Why, or why not?

2. If you haven't set up a financial workshop with a knowledge-able steward in one of the prior sessions, the end of the group might be a good time to do so. Find someone, either within or outside the group, who would be willing to provide instruction, advice, and patience to others who need help mastering money.

3. Pair up with someone from your group and think through an accountability plan. Perhaps you'll help one another save for a future expenditure or stick to a monthly budget. You may want to call each other weekly or plan to get together to go over stewardship struggles.

Note: If the group wants to continue and proceed with the same topic, consider choosing one of the books listed on page 96 (or you may want to flip back to session 1 or session 6 for more resources). The group could read one together while practicing some of the stewardship principles you've been exploring.

▼ ▼ ▼ ▼ ▼ ▼ ▼ ▼ ▼ ▼ ▼ ▼ ▼ ▼ ▼ ▼ ▼ ▼ ▼
Prayer   5 minutes

Thank God for what you're grateful for in the group. Ask for His continued guidance as the group decides whether to continue, and for relationships that have formed in the group. Thank Him for the resources He has given you. If you're comfortable, let each person complete this statement: "I'm grateful, Father, for the way this group has revealed _____ to me." This revelation may or may not have to do with money.

▼ ▼ ▼ ▼ ▼ ▼ ▼ ▼ ▼ ▼ ▼ ▼ ▼ ▼ ▼ ▼ ▼ ▼ ▼ ▼

Reference Notes

Setting: After denouncing the Pharisees (11:14-54), Jesus finds Himself before "many thousands" who gathered to hear Him preach, so many in fact that they were stepping on each other (12:1). The contrast between Christ's condemnation of the Pharisees for their selfishness and His loving concern for those truly seeking God emerges in this passage. When asked to decide a legal matter of inheritance, Jesus seizes the opportunity to remind us of what matters most, a theme He consistently teaches.

Self, Fool: The rich man is a large landowner and needs to plan for the future. But notice this basis of his logic—it's all self-directed, grounded in his life on earth with no consideration beyond. In fact, in verses 17-19, the personal pronouns for "I," "my," or "self" appear a dozen times. This is why God considered him a fool—the man can't see beyond his own barnful of grain and goods. This echoes Psalm 14:1: "The fool says in his heart, 'There is no God'" the (NIV). Despite the complexities of life, perhaps here we see that the bottom line, our ultimate direction—Self or God—reflects our ability, or inability, to see.

this subject: Although the conversation shifts from the parable of the rich man to instruction on anxiety, the content remains the same: shortsightedness versus kingdom-vision.

ravens: Jesus used three comparisons from nature—ravens (verse 24), wildflowers (often translated as lilies, verse 27), and fields (grasses of the field, verse 28). Each of them would be considered insignificant and worthless to His listeners, especially the ravens, a prolific species of crow inhabiting Palestine, considered unclean and annoying by most Jews. Jesus' comparison emphasized His point: If God cares about these things that we regularly disregard and overlook, how much more He must care for His children.

relax, preoccupied: Jesus exhorted His listeners not to worry in a present imperative Greek verb form. This stresses that He meant a consistent attitude as well as the fact that He's commanding us, not merely suggesting, that we relax by faith. His word choice implies that if we truly seek the Father, then we will learn to worry less and relax more as we exercise our faith more and more. We're free to be good stewards because God lovingly takes care of us and also uses us regularly to take care of each other.

▼ ▼ ▼ ▼ ▼ ▼ ▼ ▼ ▼ ▼ ▼ ▼ ▼ ▼ ▼ ▼ ▼ ▼ ▼ ▼

Additional Resources

The Lifetime Book of Money Management, 3rd edition, Grace W. Weinstein (Washington, D.C.: Gale Research, 1993).

Lifebalance: How to Simplify and Bring Harmony to Your Everyday Life, Linda and Richard Eyre (New York: Fireside/Simon & Schuster, 1997).

The Simple Living Guide: A Sourcebook for Less Stressful, More Joyful Living, Janet Luhrs (New York: Broadway Books, 1997).

Money Management for Those Who Don't Have Any, James L. Paris (Eugene, OR: Harvest House, 1997).

The Holy Use of Money, John C. Haughey (New York: Crossroad, 1992).

The Tightwad Gazettes, Vols. I, II, & III, Amy Dacyczyn (New York: Villard Books, 1996).

The Poverty of Affluence, Paul Wachtel (Philadelphia: New Society Publishing, 1989).

Living the Simple Life, Elaine St. James (New York: Hyperion, 1994).

Money, Sex, and Power: The Challenge of the Disciplined Life, Richard J. Foster (New York: Harper & Row, 1985).

---

1. Brother Ugolino di Monte Santa Maria, *The Little Flowers of Saint Francis,* trans. Raphael Brown (Garden City, NY: Image Books, 1958), pp. 222, 227. Cited in Richard J. Foster, *Money, Sex, and Power: The Challenge of the Disciplined Life* (New York: Harper & Row, 1985), pp. 5-6.

2. Foster, p. 37.